# IT'S
# THANKSGIVING

by JACK PRELUTSKY
pictures by
MARYLIN HAFNER

GREENWILLOW BOOKS  ·  NEW YORK

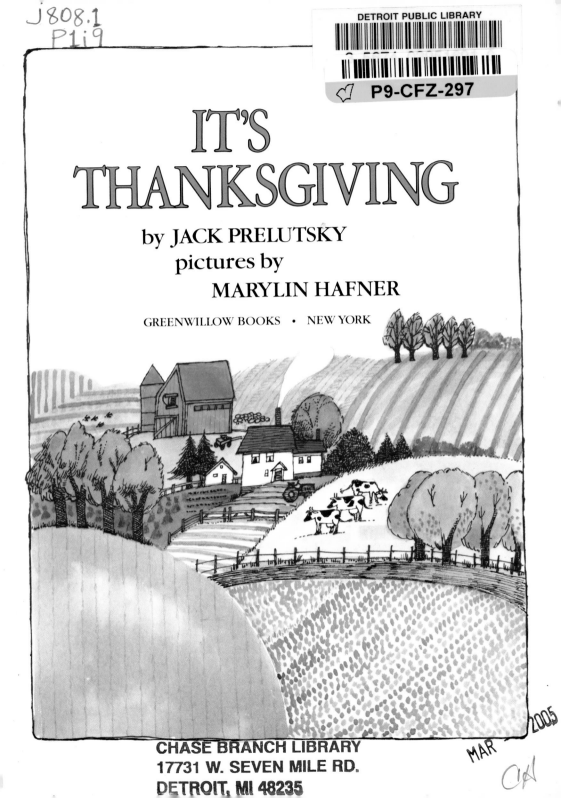

Greenwillow
Read·alone

It's Thanksgiving
Text copyright © 1982 by Jack Prelutsky
Illustrations copyright © 1982 by Marylin Hafner
Manufactured in China.
www.harperchildrens.com
First Edition 20 19 18 17 16 15

Library of Congress Cataloging in Publication Data
Prelutsky, Jack.  It's Thanksgiving.
(Greenwillow read-alone books)
Summary: Presents twelve poems about Thanksgiving, including
"When Daddy Carves the Turkey," "I Ate Too Much,"
"Daddy's Football Game," and "If Turkeys Thought."
1. Thanksgiving Day—Juvenile poetry.
2. Children's poetry, American.
[1. Thanksgiving Day—Poetry.
2. American poetry] I. Hafner, Marylin.
II. Title. III. Series.
PS3566.R36I84   811'.54   81-1929
ISBN 0-688-00441-5   AACR2
ISBN 0-688-00442-3 (lib. bdg.)
ISBN 0-688-14729-1 (pbk.)

For my brother
–J. P.

For Everett, with love
–M. H.

# CONTENTS

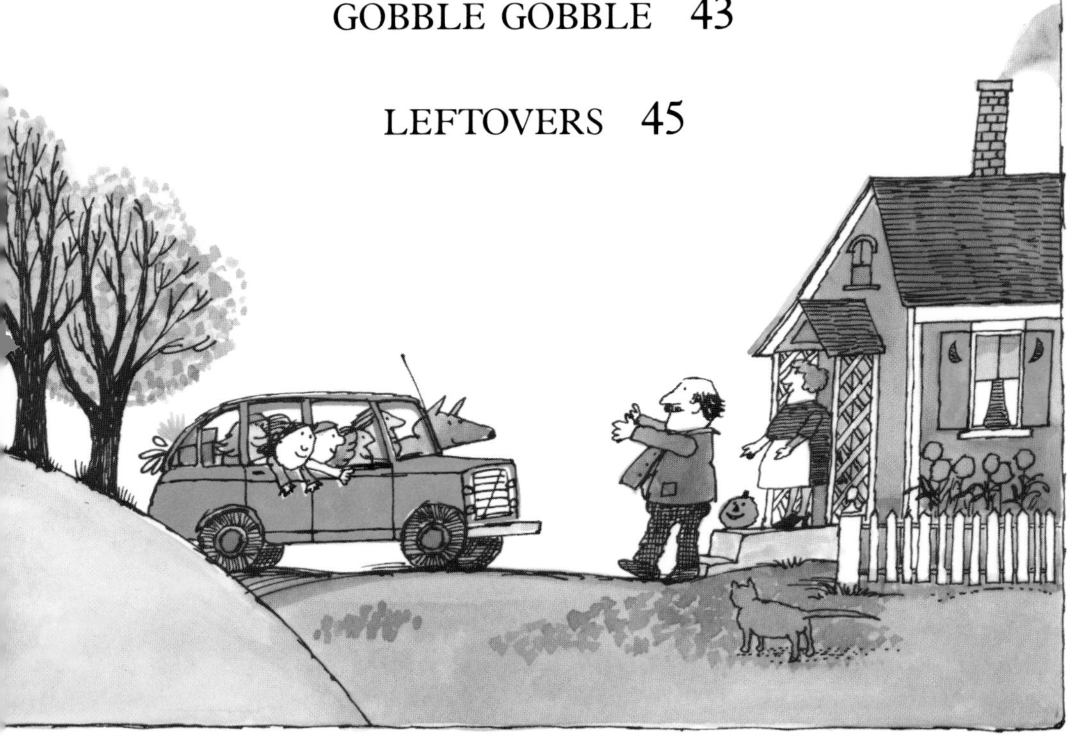

## IT'S HAPPY THANKSGIVING

It's happy Thanksgiving,
Thanksgiving! Hooray!
We're going to dinner
at Grandma's today.
I love it at Grandma's,
it's cozy and snug,
I love giving Grandma
a Thanksgiving hug.

I help make the gravy,

I pour and I stir,

it smells so delicious,

I love helping her.

We laugh and we talk,
oh! she makes such a fuss
as she bustles about
cooking dinner for us.

When we sit at the table
and Daddy says grace,
there's a beautiful smile
on my grandmother's face.

Though the weather is windy
and chilly and gray,
our family is happy
this Thanksgiving day.

# THE FIRST
# THANKSGIVING

When the Pilgrims
first gathered together to share
with their Indian friends
in the mild autumn air,
they lifted their voices
in jubilant praise
for the bread on the table,
the berries and maize,

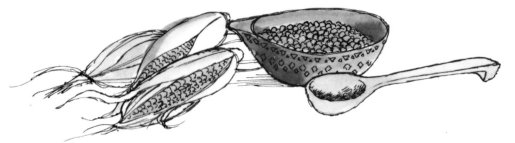

for field and for forest,

for turkey and deer,

for the bountiful crops

they were blessed with that year.

They were thankful for these
as they feasted away,
and as they were thankful,
we're thankful today.

# THE MIDDLE OF NOVEMBER

It's the middle of November
and the weather's crisp and cool,
Thanksgiving's getting closer
so there's lots to do at school.
Our teacher gives us projects
that we work on every day,
we make Indians and Pilgrims
out of paper, paste, and clay.

Our bright Thanksgiving murals
are displayed on all the walls,
and our cut-out paper pumpkins
gaily decorate the halls.

Today I drew a turkey
with a fat and funny face–
in the middle of November
school's a very busy place.

## IF TURKEYS THOUGHT

If turkeys thought, they'd run away
a week before Thanksgiving Day,
but turkeys can't anticipate,
and so there's turkey on my plate.

# I WENT HUNGRY
# ON THANKSGIVING

I was hungry on Thanksgiving,
but I couldn't eat a thing,
I couldn't eat a drumstick
and I couldn't eat a wing,

I couldn't have the pickles

or the gravy-covered rice,

the pumpkin pie was luscious,

but I couldn't have a slice.

I was starving for some stuffing

or a tasty yellow yam,

or a puffy little muffin

spread with homemade berry jam.

Our dinner looked delicious,

but I didn't dare to touch,

I went hungry on Thanksgiving—

my new braces hurt so much.

# THE THANKSGIVING DAY PARADE

Thanksgiving Day is here today,
the great parade is under way,
and though it's drizzling quite a bit,
I'm sure that I'll see all of it.

Great balloons are floating by,
cartoon creatures stories high,
Mickey Mouse and Mother Goose,
Snoopy and a mammoth moose.

Humpty Dumpty, Smokey Bear
hover in the autumn air,
through the windy skies they sway,
I hope that they don't blow away.

Here comes Santa, shaking hands
as he waddles by the stands.
It's so much fun, I don't complain
when now it *really* starts to rain.

The bands are marching, here they come,

pipers pipe and drummers drum,

hear the tubas and the flutes,

see the clowns in silly suits.

It's pouring now, but not on me,

I'm just as dry as I can be,

I watch and watch, but don't get wet,

I'm watching on our TV set.

## WHEN DADDY
## CARVES THE TURKEY

When Daddy carves the turkey,
it is really quite a sight,
I know he tries his hardest,
but he never does it right.

He makes a fancy show of it
before he starts to carve,
and stabs in all directions
while we're certain that we'll starve.

He seems to take forever
as we sit and shake our heads,
by the time he's finished slicing
he's reduced the bird to shreds.

He yells as loud as thunder
just before he's finally through
for when Daddy carves the turkey,
Daddy carves his finger too.

# I ATE TOO MUCH

I ate too much turkey,
I ate too much corn,
I ate too much pudding and pie,
I'm stuffed up with muffins
and much too much stuffin',
I'm probably going to die.

I piled up my plate

and I ate and I ate,

but I wish I had known when to stop,

for I'm so crammed with yams,

sauces, gravies, and jams

that my buttons are starting to pop.

I'm full of tomatoes

and french fried potatoes,

my stomach is swollen and sore,

but there's still some dessert,

so I guess it won't hurt

if I eat just a little bit more.

## DADDY'S FOOTBALL GAME

Our turkey dinner's hardly gone
when Daddy says, "The game is on."

He tunes it in, takes off his shoes,
and turns to watch his heroes lose.

He seems to take it very hard
whenever they fall short a yard.
"Another incomplete," he grunts,
"more penalties, more bungled punts."

"They're missing tackles," Daddy mumbles,
"dropping passes, making fumbles. . . .
INTERCEPTION!" Daddy roars,
as once again the wrong team scores.

He sits and screams, we sit and grin,
he gets so mad when they don't win.
Thanksgiving wouldn't be the same
without my father's football game.

# THE
# WISHBONE

Wishbone, wishbone
on a dish,
pick it up
and make a wish.
If I pull
the wishbone right,
I will get
my wish tonight.

Wishbone, wishbone,
will I win?
Will I laugh
and clap and grin?
When the wishbone
snaps in two,
will my wishbone
wish come true?

Wishbone, wishbone,
now it snaps,
my sister grins
and laughs and claps.
Wishbone, wishbone,
I don't laugh,
my sister got
the bigger half.

## GOBBLE GOBBLE

When the turkey gobble gobbles,
it is plump and proud and perky,
when our family gobble gobbles,
we are gobbling down the turkey.

# LEFTOVERS

Thanksgiving has been over
for at least a week or two,
but we're still all eating turkey,
turkey salad, turkey stew,

turkey puffs and turkey pudding,
turkey patties, turkey pies,
turkey bisque and turkey burgers,
turkey fritters, turkey fries.

For lunch our mother made us
turkey slices on a stick,
there'll be turkey tarts for supper,
all this turkey makes me sick.

For tomorrow she's preparing
turkey dumplings stuffed with peas,
oh I never thought I'd say this–
"Mother! No more turkey . . . PLEASE!"

## JACK PRELUTSKY

was born and raised in New York City and now lives in Albuquerque, New Mexico. His popular books for children include *The Queen of Eene, The Snopp on the Sidewalk,* and *Nightmares* (all ALA Notable Books), *The Headless Horseman Rides Tonight,* and *Rolling Harvey down the Hill.* He is also the author of three other Greenwillow Read-alone Books illustrated by Marylin Hafner: *It's Christmas, It's Halloween,* and *Rainy Rainy Saturday.*

## MARYLIN HAFNER

studied at Pratt Institute and the School of Visual Arts in New York City. She has illustrated many distinguished picture books, including *Big Sisters Are Bad Witches* by Morse Hamilton. Among the Greenwillow Read-alone Books she has illustrated are *Mind Your Manners* by Peggy Parish, *Camp KeeWee's Secret Weapon* and *Jenny and the Tennis Nut* by Janet Schulman, and *Mrs. Gaddy and the Ghost* by Wilson Gage. Ms. Hafner lives in Cambridge, Massachusetts.